Last Harvest

ALSO BY HARRY GUEST

POETRY
A Different Darkness
Arrangements
The Cutting-Room
The Achievements of Memory
Mountain Journal
A House Against the Night
The Hidden Change
Elegies (2nd edition, 2018*)
Lost and Found
Coming to Terms
So Far
A Puzzling Harvest (*Collected Poems 1955–2000*)
Comparisons & Conversions *
Some Times
Short Attention Span *

NOVELS
Days
Lost Pictures
Time After Time
The Light and the Smoke

RADIO PLAYS
The Inheritance
The Emperor of Outer Space

TRANSLATIONS
Post-War Japanese Poetry (*with Lynn Guest and Kajima Shôzô*)
The Distance, The Shadows (*66 Poems by Victor Hugo*)
Versions
From a Condemned Cell (*33 Sonnets by Jean Cassou*)
A Square in East Berlin (*a novel by Torsten Schulz*)
Otherlands *

NON-FICTION
Another Island Country
Mastering Japanese
Traveller's Literary Companion to Japan
The Artist on the Artist

* *published by Shearsman Books*

Harry Guest

LAST HARVEST

Shearsman Books

First published in the United Kingdom in 2020 by
Shearsman Books Ltd
PO Box 4239
Swindon
SN3 9FN

Shearsman Books Ltd Registered Office
30–31 St. James Place, Mangotsfield, Bristol BS16 9JB
(this address not for correspondence)

www.shearsman.com

ISBN 978-1-84861-726-1

CONTENTS

2175 A.D.

no. tu.wun.sen.five. wee.do.not.yooz.long.wurdz.
yoo.kan.not.say.twen.tee.wun.fow.zand.or.sev.enn.
a.d.is.rong.tu. wee.yooz.wurdz.not.a.b.c.
at.skul.wee.lern.short.wurdz.wiv.just.wun.sownd.
zer.wuns.hoo.teech.us.du.not.no.yuze.long.wurdz.
no.wun.duz.
wen.wee.leev.skul.wee.go.to.kol.if.wee.ar.brite.
wee.lern.vare.how.to.sel.fingz.
how.do.wee.sel.fingz.
wee.say.vis.iz.ur.kup. cee.it. bie.it. vat.iz.ur.kar. bie.it.
ven.vay.say.how.mutch.
five.pownz.or.ten.pownz.plus.for.pownz.or.nine.tenz.plus.ait.pownz.
vare.ar.just.free.noatz. wun.wunz.five.wunz.ten.wunz.
at.kol.yoo.hav.tu.pay.ten.bie.ten.bie.ten.pownz.eetch.yer.
wee.ar.at.kol.for.free.yerz.
yes.ur.lot.ov.kash.
it.is.kwite.hard.to.cownt.in.wunz.and.fivze.and.tenz.
wee.hav.no.bux. vay.woz.awl.bernt.yers.bak.

haitch.gest.rote.it.

A Paragraph from Mallarmé's *Crise de Vers*

I say two words – "a flower" – and from
the depths of sheer oblivion as
my voice consigns there contours like
curved outlines other than blooms known,
arising musically and suave,
concept itself identifies
the one not there in all bouquets.

Stone Islands

B.C.

One mile-long chasm tilting to the sea
scraped for millennia by springs, downpours
and time. Dry now.
           At the parched mouth
above some curling waves storm-petrels whirr
outside this so-called grotto. One huge leg
of limestone stamped in to these hardly ever tides
to cause a cave never inhabited
like elsewhere long ago, a given space
of ecstasy, blue mirror shimmering for
a beckoning sun.
           Between this standpoint and
horizon juts a danger-isle far-flung,
the fifth one in the archipelago
named Filfla, rarely visited, too barren.
           Back,
up left, along the cliffs, two temples wait
built there before the pyramids, before
Stonehenge, much added to from centuries
to next. All hefty stones, some giant slabs
bigger than wardrobes and far heavier,
dragged to the sites it's thought upon round stones
not logs, not many trees to waste, half-inched
by inch, then further, roped perhaps, pulled, that's
enough, phew (mopping brow), wait for new sun
and start again, no hurry.
           Quâ phallic (really?)
sloping slightly, two tall pillars hinting at
a doorway or a gate to emptiness.
Once inside, enclosed, lesser trilithons

offer sometimes an entrance to low altars
for what to whom.
                Some orthostats have holes
and, wider, "letter-box-slits" for
delivery of what again – food? gifts?
objects in homage? pottery? figurines? Who
across the æons can decide. At times
a tiny gap prised out might just allow
a shaft of sunrise through at winter solstice
or midsummer dawn to hit the further wall.
It's all conjecture, pliable, of interest though
all stays unproved.
                How did the builders come?
From where (when's known) and why? To slay
all pygmy elephants who'd grazed there for so long?
Escape from enemies? Pushed off in exile?
To find somewhere that's not as far as where
the sea's finality ends tumbling down
to nothingness?

A.D.

                Some coasts spread broken areas
harsh underfoot but genuinely fine
to stumble over, hearing waves some five
feet lower lap, see lizards vanish in
a flick. No gulls surprisingly. Too far
to fly for scavenging? Unlikely. Pools
in sunlight dry so fast they leave
pale salt where water was. Given the long-
drawn hard unwelcome rock small wonder that
the travelling apostle got shipwrecked.
We had the privilege of watching his
dark distant statue underneath the sun-

set each evening across the bay.

Elsewhere
quasi-forgotten fields and rough stone walls
stagger down slopes to keep the earth and grass.
Two sorts of limestone underneath and used.
Coralline's durable. Smooth yellow slabs
are easier to cut.

These days and sadly
there's more "development" as on
the Channel Isles, less landscapes than
there used to be. Yes people have to live
somewhere. Roofs over heads. Hotels
for tourists like ourselves. There's no
solution but all could be well without
unworthy millionaires and second homes
filled just a week or two per year.

Grey on the land.
Thick heat each noon. Uninterrupted azure
overhead. One town upon a hill is called
the silent one. These streets of golden stone
disappear intriguingly round curves too
narrow happily for traffic. A sort
of loveliness, a kind of calm. Church towers
bristle from parishes. Each cross, a plus,
gives eight enlightening rays out. On a shield
a prancing horse bright red would like to reach
the crescent moon. A rebus probably.
Which language?

Well, we surely will one day
set out aglow again and possibly return
with nothing less than zero. Now we leave
the darkest blue of sea patched here
and there with green that lies a while
or swirls. One falcon glimpsed, inland.
Some red-capped sparrows in a hedge.

                                        To go
back home with dreams and photographs
taking some wonders barely understood
to ponder on at dusk beside the fire,
pass over snow draping the Alps and take
at last the train from Gatwick skimming past
thick foliage and running water once
again.

on Malta and Gozo, April 2016

Stones Set

for Tilla Brading and Frances Presley

To glance away after so many
years – decades – those three moors explored
with others or alone, streams to cross
or follow, strange woods far apart
some not pathed, all dense, thick, once a fox
turning the corner – pause – decides
to leave, tors in snow climbed gingerly,
deer's footprint, splash of water down a hill
below an Iron Age forge now silent,
tall wall of fog ahead blue sky warm
on your nape, large space of bare rock,
one April cuckoos heard north distance,
east and south nearer, one seen east close
flit from ash to single tree, buzzard above,
the openness, in season flowers, sense
almost of eternity although to
be back in time for tea, rest, bath,
recall the wind, clouds changing colour,
sheets of rain and sun, the miniliths
and higher, split with frost, leaning
in softer soil, may fall, patterned in rows
or circles, placed far earlier than
the pyramids, less massive than
Stonehenge or Avebury,
enough however here for mysteries,
times to get lost on, found again,
a different beauty, wilder, spread, bare and
always the past put there in stone to stay

Where To and From *or* Back to Back

Back to the middle ages… Did they know
what they lay in the centre of? Say dark
on one flank, triple-pre-post-modern on
the nearer i.e. us. We must recall
how savagery got dubbed crusades, condemn
the vicious acts of Tudors, take a breath
and shift to ponderous angles of what brought
enlightenment. Those shadowed eras haunt
the ages Chesterton defined so well
as "Christian killeth Christian" not unlike
some decades in our recent past.
                                All seems
to go wrong easily. So much to mourn
for when the Holy Ghost plus Jesus plead
for peace and harmony, forgiveness, love,
compassion. Not too difficult.
                                In Psalms
the Father (ours for some) seems to have strayed
from utter beauty crossed with common-sense
to smiting, bloodshed, warfare, just a hope
for help against both enemy and sin.
Starvation too. In truth the focus stays
firm for creation, comfort, "portion", works
and wisdom – intermittent beams sent from
a verbal lighthouse there for guiding while
we so-called humans vitiated most
of what religions are about e.g.
fresh wonder, the unknown drawn nearer, faith
as hints for life, a way to climb that slope
which looked so hard and turn frustration to
another type of curve.

                    Religion should
be flexible, no proselytising, your
religion might not suit his, hers or mine.
All must refrain from violence, admit
the presence of all others, find some queer
perhaps (why not?) but smile and tolerate,
treating humanity with equal calm.
Think X a kind of mirror of yourself
unless of course you learn of theft, drugs, fraud
and prejudice but they're not really all
that common. Yet.
                    We sadly know some thrive
on terror. There exists a vile sect still
pretending there's a pseudo-deity,
a counterfeit, a dirty sham who wants
what's been created wrecked, what's right ignored,
what's innocent destroyed, a man who loves
a man hurled to his death. To train a lad
of fourteen how to mix inside a crowd
minding their business then let off a bomb
so he'll be blown to smithereens along
with families who may (may not) believe
the drivel he'd been coaxed to – is this brand
of horror a *religious* way of life?
Teaching a younger boy to shoot to kill
some prisoners makes it certain he'll end up
a slaughterer impossible to cure
or aid. Will those two pass eternity
beneath the flaring skies of hell? Maybe
with thugs who made them monsters far before
their years which wouldn't happen anyway.
The twisters who watch torture gloatingly,
plan murders, live on hatred can't deserve
the privileged title "human", ever know
what a religion is these latter days

when certain faults condemned do not exist
now.
      Prayer's a good initiative if there's
a recognized intention sent from self
to elsewhere. Disappointments come of course.
And vanish, surely that's the point, each prayer
by only seeming ineffectual
threads like a submarine through solid land
below the kneeler inexplicably
and tends to alter into something not
foreseen. A lesson in a sense for one
can't tell God what to do. What's needed is
a flag more like a rainbow under which
we'll free the chains of fear, hope soon there'll shine
a sacred epoch to eradicate
these evils so they'll never slither back.

A Dream

I wandered in distress somewhere alone
and noticed nothing anywhere save for
a string of clouds darker than yesterdays,
unthought of now wherever now may be.

Now hangs on glances to each side though mist
blurred looking further – like a trudge across
the moor when, suddenly, lines of grey stone
set upright you'd gone by will vanish while

the rise ahead holds for a time a height
as one horizon – like a brink past which
a gulf might yawn of denser fog not to
plunge into now or later. Then I felt

a moisture trickling on my cheeks like tears
I hadn't shed as yet. Those chasms in
my brain filch names and words away. They lose
what used to flicker from my tongue with ease

replacing badinage with silence, themes
with walls of soot, true learning with a void.
That's why the sleeping pilgrim has to keep
his pacing till dawn choruses occur

and, banishing the stroll to nowhere, prove
fragments remain which may not glow enough –
the way ahead will fade away, this dream
convey no message but a lasting fear.

Discoveries Along the Distant North

six golden days in Norway with my son Nick

A map of fjords for one no seaman seems
enticing though a kind of spider's web –
so many islands in so many shapes,
so many inlets curving even east
at times. So chuck away the atlas and
explore reality.
                              Mysterious hills
and distant isles for dawn's imagining
slide past what seems a different planet, rock
so unfamiliar passing by a low
grey coast, no beach, stone thrust in water, more
than hard to wander on in dreams beyond
another hidden lake or opening for
a stretch of other water for the sea,
then possibly watch islands turn into
a long peninsula as other streams
arrive or leave each way.
                              Also the sun
at noon or dusk beams where it shouldn't be
like hints of there or even where. The ship
steers in a maze when rivers on the left-
hand side might shift alternately to join
or go so slowly that you can't decide
which way is which.
                              Too pointless to connect
river to river – each one's rushed, tossed white,
while others, also wide, stay calm – so dark,
so silent, held between huge sides of rock
raised almost vertical, now splashed with snow
(it's May) in patches. Several long thin lines

of frozen water from each highest wall
fall to an apparent lake. Some seem to melt
already trickling and of course all those
immense and heavy waterfalls like clouds
that always roar, hurl spray around, crash down.
You flow on slowly, later pass below
a threatening canyon, sunless sometimes, quite
as sinister as still.
                    Trees of all kinds
grow perilously on long narrow paths,
bare cliff above and under. Tops of hills
gone mountains now retain a smear of snow
that stays a while perhaps in jagged black
or smooths of curve.
                    Edges along the fjords
allow roads to get built but when long cliffs
continue down in water then they need
some tunnels burrowed. We've been told one twists
for seven kilometres in darkness till
a tiny prick of light grows on ahead
to gain that deep and tranquil mirror like
a lake that heads eventually to meet
the sea.
          High on the plateau (endless rolls
of mountain under thicker snow in May)
a slope of stones resembles years ago
a glacier falling. It's a dam to hold
the cold, wide pool behind it and create
a lot of electricity, don't ask
how, merely nod our heads in wonder, look
in rapture where the sky's turned upside down
without a sign of human work around –
no pylons, no advertisements, no pipes,
no traffic-lights, no chimneys, hence no make-
belief.

Along the road stand tall sticks put
along each side for miles and miles to guide
all passers-by in heavy snow, past too
a little building. You can stop and choose
a plate of waffles.
                              There's a village with
a broader hurrying river pouring down
a steepish hill with heavy waves of white,
also a fjord which looks as placid as
a lake surrounded by a landscape so
it can't escape. However, we came here
from the North Sea by ship to prove the weird
control of turbulence and easy flow.
Here's a museum, hanging portraits and
fine pictures of each vista. Soaring cliffs
insist both east and west must wait till sun-
shine and the moon in full (with stars) peer down
on open space for pleasure kept so clean
(unlike alas the England of to-day)
where you can see a metal vixen and
her cub, find benches you can sit on, see
an ancient yellow house reflected in
the almost still dark water turned to bronze
in later sunlight. You can stroll along
this frothing stream for miles, admire the height
of forest on your left and if you need
to speak must try a shout.
                              Nearer the sea
the oldest church in Norway closed inside
her grass-green rectangle's been overdone.
A pity. Anyway. Up from the ship
that's waiting there's a bistro with a lunch
for Nick and me (good beer and lots of cheese
though quite expensive; not to worry on
a holiday) and higher up a church

we hoped to enter and absorb the signs
of faith inside a land we hadn't seen
before but in the door a man would not
allow us in unless we paid a sum.
Yes. Churches must get money, one should leave
some coins or crackling paper in the well-
seen slots set in the wall but it's not right
to treat a sacred building like a zoo,
some royal house or exhibitions. In
cathedrals you must usually pay
because you're there as tourists but they leave
a chapel open just before you pay
so you can pray then leave if you don't want
to see those coloured windows telling facts
or inspiration, naves and altars, fonts,
a vault in curves of stone, a chance to read
some possibly exaggerated words
on tombs of famous people you might know
or not.
A graveyard just above a town
in total spring blazed with the flowers on trees
which line paths round all squares of grass for graves
surrounded by a fence of thicker hedge
raised higher in each corner as a care-
ful guardian. All creates true calm and peace,
yes sorrow realistically and known
like understanding death accepted as
a truth in time. Then there are special squares
for Norway's patriots and soldiers brought
from overseas in World War Two to die
too young in foreign earth. You sense concern,
great gratitude, knowledge of waste, those years
of pointlessness like any war.
Walls here
and elsewhere on the ways you go are built

with bulky stones meticulously, no
concrete no mortar used so you can see
few sparks of light beneath a careful roof
of grass that's smoothing the effect.
                                    Down on
the spreading water on a small tree'd hill
three lengthy swords (some fifteen feet high) stand
stuck in the ground to memorize long long
ago the Vikings who'd found much, it must
be recognized in violence, to find
a world of wonder round those distant worlds
of difference.
                        Few birds above. Some swans
in rivers. Smaller seagulls than we'd known.
One buzzard whirling slowly round the top
of unsnowed mountains. In the fields sheep, lambs,
black horses, cows. Most people in the streets
on May their seventeenth wore costumes, dark
and from the past.
                            Such luck in weather. They
explain in joke each year means nine wet months
of rain and three cold months of snow. I did,
when sailing here from Dover, nearly fall
from bed at two a.m. as waves quite high
with splashing on the porthole helped the ship
to roll this way and that. I reached at last
a fascinating land I'd always craved
to see and day by day the sky stayed blue
and walking round this grand strange country made
things warm and clear.
                                Not knowing what the end
of travelling inside the fjords could feel
like, one delightful shock of pleasantry
occurred along a low coast on the way
away to west. Grey rock unique in tones

of colour like the cliffs and stones we'd been
examining for a week looked rather hard
to scramble on no more than forty feet
above the water. Not a treat now though
this would have been for me decades before
so seeing them provided easily
a kind of melancholy to say farewell.

Romantic

At home nowhere but happy here
or there when things look settled
for a while – only a while
since otherwhere is always beckoning,
the grass more emerald, windows
far brighter, stars relied on.

To-morrows come though not in vain.
Rain only falls between the stroke of mid-
night and pre-daybreak. When you've been too
long somewhere restlessness sets in and you're
away again and no-one can
Identify the destination, that's the key.

A Walk with Nick Along the Cliffs

Such pleasure. Circling three hours round. Sky just
pale grey not moving. To the south across
the lower land not seeing sea at first.
A river on the right before a view
to the horizon with the Channel dark,
quiet blue. Beyond a line of dead-white clouds
(pretending to look like some further hills)
ran from the opposite of eastern Lyme
to west descent of Devon to its low-
est part. We passed eight people, several dogs
and one old lady on her horse. All kept
so quiet (not the canines) as we trudged
in pure delight down slopes up higher ones
watching them losing calm sea as the coast
dipped underneath itself.
                       From time to time
the sun we never saw above us shone
in faint gold on a distant valley sliced
to fields of flat apparent warmth (in some
no kidding there are llamas). It's a day
well mostly afternoon you can't forget,
breathing the salt, hearing a lark's song or
shrill *keeps* from oystercatchers far below,
pausing at times to talk or glance down at
smooth vivid pebbles made that way in swirls
for untold years of sea till tides fell back,
left stones on sand for countless time then once
more lifted them to moor and sunlight, high,
uncovered, waiting there.

After April

It's early day, the daisies haven't yet
opened, the western way, no-one against
the sun sees anything except where one
yew drops darkness on thin faded grass near
bluebells some ramsons fighting over drifts
of paler white, azure far denser. Soon,
in June, there won't be any anyway.

Further, sadly, a Red Admiral's bright wing
caught between two pebbles, loss unexplained
of beauty fluttering in sunlight if
no leaves could catch the falling beams then shed
new shadow on the earth beneath. The rain
may even differences of tone and leave
a glitter here and there

And After Afterwards

that shift to minor darkening the pleasure
which must come back although
a certain sadness hangs around
will hang   no other option

recital over   much applause
enthusiastic chat   small glass of wine

and then the semblance of a walk
all sounds
all scattered sounds

mind elsewhere for
reality's too slippery to catch

the glance of someone
force of oboes or
precise curls of a lily plus the cold
stroll on each November street

in a novel doomed possibly
or not such matters coalesce aside
some consequence which makes no sense
a full moon mirrored as a square

and then that dream in twilight
figure clad in sombre cloth
and heading down
away a narrow avenue between
snow-covered trees

"Before Abraham came to be, I *am*."

(Rieu's translation of John VIII, v.58)

It's claimed "God spake these words and said" for when
we *speak* we do not necessarily
say what's important, comic or sublime.
Words often flow to no avail, just show
you're there, still conscious, friendly like, about
to walk on silently and leave a trace
of attitude behind – but if you say
"I'll be there" then you *will* be otherwise
you're unreliable and when God said
"Don't slay" He meant it so don't steal or lie,
look after Mum and Dad, stay on good terms
with neighbours even if they're fractious or
just boring, don't be greedy, say your prayers,
ignore false gods, remember Him and go
to church. Not much to ask.
                              When Jesus told
the crowd that He'd seen Abraham He was
quite right, He had, but not the way we try
to come to terms with, it's all literally
beyond us here and now though later on
we'll know won't we.
                              When Jesus chose to mix
those tenses in John's Gospel there's a clash
between Time and Eternity which can't
make ordinary sense. The mystery
remains, is hard and fast, can't be explained.
"Before Abraham was, I am." A blaze.
A rainbowed paradox. For Jesus is
all God and at the same time is all man
which is impossible and therefore true.

Easter, 2015

Beware

The man without a shadow even though
a sun still tranquil sends rays from the east
gives orders to who'll act them lovingly
unless they've trust again that's lasting. Strange
how people passing throw their flattened shape
on paving while he stands immobile, smiles
with lips not eyes, spreads fear. To comprehend
the words for evil delve from childhood all
those midnight terrors, ask what's underneath
the bed and see if you can reach the door
unscathed. To know what monsters are is not
enough. Nor confidence. In looking back
ensure no camouflaged deceit lies on
the path to trip you, send you sprawling, flaunt
a knife then vanish. You're the only one
who saw threat, flash of steel, heard promise hissed
about returns no indication of,
nor hint of warning, no escape, the end
assured however long the stretch of one
strayed future keeps it tentatively far
to make those strung-up tortures last. When each
reversal of some slick criterion,
one or the other, will take charge once more
to horrify. Yes, you're correct. Much could
occur and after all the shadow may,
who knows, one afternoon appear, a set
of blackened wings between which hard to see
the figure droops, a ghost with face of fire.

"Beyond These Slightly Misted Hills..."

Beyond these slightly misted hills
one long grey cloud behaving like
a distant range itself has formed
far off a new geography
six thousand feet at least of slope
till any climber could have reached
a non-existent line of peaks
all curved and letting eyes surprised
to see past low horizons we're
so used to
            to perhaps a sea
scattered with unknown islands cliffed
quite high, no beaches probably
all round, hard to explore but are
we meant to try them? should we leave
that teasing archipelago
alone? such darkened mountains must
scurry away by evening, it's
not worth to mourn the absence of
a new delight intriguing one
who would look up and could believe
what isn't likely for a while
of pleasure, wait with patience week
by week in hoping different sights
might turn up to delude and bring
new ideas set from other skies

Conversation

Come die with me, the lover said.
No, no, the other man replied –
I live a double life, need to
be cautious not dramatic. *I*
see you and her each afternoon
walk arm in arm along the deck.
It hurts me, makes me fear you don't
desire me any longer, won't
recall the way you held me to
you, said in gasps you can't survive
without my kisses. Yes, of course,
I love your naked body close
to mine, your lips exploring me.
When writhing skilfully in bed
or elsewhere we know each one needs
the other's pleasure and his skill.
I want you in my cabin, nude
and eager like the last times. This
is not a cruiser! Solid ground!
Between a bus stop and the park
with flowers and fountains. *We're now on*
the ship of life where everyone
seeks love. And secrecy. You said
come die with you. Does that imply
we meet, strip, kiss, stroke, lick, enjoy
each other to the spurting then
quite casually pick two guns
up, smile then shoot ourselves? Who first?
And will the second fire? Or do
we drink some speedy poison like
Vilikins and his Dinah and

get buried in the same grave? *If
two lovers love together but
one knows it's the last time does he
acknowledge it? A parting must
resemble death, the sadness, end,
so, when we come again for love
don't tell me till you say Good-bye.*

Cosmos
for Kevin Bailey who scans the skies

For all we know the universe
out there may not be there at all.
We can be relatively sure
a certain star – Kerb, Nath, Arkab
Posterior, gamma Cos or one
of those our forebears dubbed *king star,*
day of the sungod, stormy bird –
stood hurtling on in space just where
it used to be so many light
years back. That stream of brightness on
its usual way to-day may leave
increasing blackness in its wake.
Turned into starsmoke now, the source,
blaze, lux intensity will not
get lit again. Our sun could have
minutes ago burnt out to let
us float in icy darkness from
now on. As for the galaxies –
what is five hundred thousand times
six million million miles? for that's
how far some of them are, immense
bee-clusters of self-distant stars
impossible to think of yet
they're there or may have vanished some
twelve thousand years before. We see
as legends through our telescopes
a long-forgotten trace of light
from unimaginable dark.
One day or far off century
our shepherd Helios alone
in endless nothingness may keep

familiar planets spinning round
and satellites revolving with
more Greek names happening all the time
but once the sun has set there'll still
be Venus but no starlight just
unfathomable blackness past
our moon, each night as deep as lack
of hope, as vacant as a child's
idea of prison, leaving us
to mourn the nightly glitter with
star-absence looming and to fear
the soon extinction of the sun.

Cymru Kernow Armor

Crossing the Tamar to sunset my Welsh blood
tingles there's a sense not of coming home but
dropping in to another land of cousins
those three rough outcrops with three sides of water
probing west have much in common, hidden woods,
fields strewn with rocks, dark cliffs blurring in rainfall

Those saints with names not quite explicable skimmed
on their millstones following perhaps the flight
of a handsome angel did they wield a pole
steering them like a coracle or rely
on prayer even a pagan magic who's to
know beyond those centuries and never why

Gold was a feature long before porphyry,
coal tunnels, clay since legends near menhirs still
trickle through clefts leading to shelves where skulls once
stared and recall the loss of islands never
found before or after though the tides may be
writing something undeciphered on cold sand

Dead All Day

A little girl, told once upon a time
her hamster Fred was dead, said "Oh" and paused
in thought, then frowned. "Will he be dead all day?"
Well, Lazarus came forth.
                              Rachmaninov's
C minor Prelude scares us with those three
descending octaves. Some macabrely claim
they represent the clods of earth which thud
down on the coffin.
                              Active music next.
The one they've wrongly buried scrabbles on
the lid in vain. No claustrophobes need try
remembering this. Or write about it either.

In Torsten Schulz's novel set in East
Berlin two old folk sitting near some graves
suggest alarms should be installed in them
after each funeral in case of false
analysis like the grim ballad penned
in doggerel by Friederike Kempner
about a child mistakenly interred.

To go back to the little girl. What could
that weird word *death* mean to her? Longer nap?
Avoidance? *"No. Don't bother Daddy now."*
A pointless veto tedious for a while?
"Your Auntie's here, you'll have to play outside."
She knows parentheses get put round time
but not the length of permanence. No-one
she's loved or didn't has just gone away
and not come back. Things change but there's no loss

except a favourite toy that's never found.
She lives in blessèd ignorance when days
recur reliably and flowers that flamed
the year before do so next spring. It's fun
to find you're growing taller though you don't
know why or care.
              Life's all around, doles out
surprise, makes odd decisions there has been
no need to brood about but sadly now
she'll have to learn what sorrow is because
Fred will stay dead all day and stay that way.

Fall back on splendour...

Fall back on splendour. It's the only way.
Stroke velvet say or just allow a kind
of darkness to resemble secrecy
and mention luxuries in case some loot's
been lent for ever as a poor excuse.

If stags with golden hooves draw phantom sleighs
(should they be needed) stay surrounded by
a quietude of stillborn dreams nightmared
again by guilt discovered earlier
from weather more reliable than love.

Or comprehension of a language. Once
its verbs get lost, one, keen on equal thought
for all, needs concepts to consider speed
since magic carpets shunning moonlight skim
between each bridge and water (mind your head).

Along far coasts how many shades of blue
are flung by clouds of differing size and height?
Huge squares of azure, navy-tinted zig-
zags, sapphired isles in two dimensions, close
to colours lacking names to haunt the sea.

Now wait for twilight. Add a further west
of dying scarlets slashed to brush the day
away with types of green on purpose for
a walker wondering how he'll step beyond
the threshold of another fantasy.

Five Stanzas on Disenchantment

A dawn wind stirs the curtains. He'll recite
some lines in silence Rimbaud scrawled in rage.
She shifts and mutters nothings from the night.
Regret stands out among the penalties of age.

In dreams he clambers up a faulty flight
of stairs where conscience, startled, learns to gauge
the length of envy. Let the bone hand write
elaborate misgivings on another page.

Two lovers lying find less appetite
for change once honeymoons have reached the stage
of perjury. One thoughtless sonnet might
release the seven leopards fretting in their cage.

Alarming strips of neon – cold blue, white –
put off the final Hamlets caught offstage.
The turmoil caused by that lax acolyte
brought down a punishment no penance could assuage.

Did Zeus reward or slay his catamite?
Now any journalist can disengage
remorse from sin, switch grief from left to right.
Only the moribund deserve a living wage.

Floors

for our son-in-law Sébastien with love

They're underneath of course throughout
time now not ceilings high between
skies spread above nor walls about
life horizontally and seen
by levelled glances, once a treat
for you. Don't look ahead inside
a room or on a city street
or anywhere that's dignified
but keep your head down, don't watch up,
check carpets, flagstones, rugs, wood tiles
beneath your feet, keep plate and cup
low on each table, in the aisles
of churches do not realise
there are those roofings. When friends come
you can't examine lips, cheeks, eyes.
Just shoes. Outside you won't succumb
to rainbows, red clouds, stars. No fall
of shower. Heard plashes on a pool.
At home no windows, mirrors, all
those pictures hung with care, books you'll
not count along your shelves until
at hospital at last they've said
facelift once more, reveal the thrill
of dangling lampshades overhead.

(composed after an operation on the author's right eye)

Forest Talk

Autumn so
the sunlight's greyer.

A non-existent gauze blurs distance
slightly. Not that you glimpse what's far till gaps
occur among the trees.
Or on the edges.
        Jays too rarely seen
keeping that vivid plumage out of sight
screech and rattle foliage.
                Then
silence once more.
          A blackbird warns
whoever's interested that one,
not bringing danger, gunless, liking birds,
is on the way.
          Quiet again.

A rook flaps indolently across a patch
of sky unbreezed, not even zephyred,
calm.
        Grey squirrels leave the faintest
patter on the grass
then scramble up an oak and disappear.

I stand still.

No sound save the September drifting of the leaves.

Gun As Vase

Two human walls.
A space between.
One side faith in napalm.
One none in this war
dragged on in vain.
(There'll be a curved
memorial
near here one day.)

A lad in jeans and t-shirt
moved across no-man's-land
towards the same fresh face,
age, height, nationality.
His khaki double.

Who held a rifle
aimed at his mirror-self.
Jittery. But prepared.

The walker came closer.
Both walls held their breath.
He stopped, inches away.
Brought a flower from behind his back.
Slid the stalk into the barrel.

The rifle now
(a horizontal vase)
                bloomed.

Effigy

St. Blaise, Haccombe

The face looks too old for sixteen –
not carefree or alert – plagued with
grown-up concerns he never lived
to learn. He's lost the sword he wore –
unswished in battle, only used
to scrape along his teacher's blade,
make silver sparks to vanish in
a flash of time. War practices.
Boar-hunts and banquets. Prayer and sleep.

Though lying down in death he stands
in alabaster on a hound
who peers up, doesn't seem to mind
his master's non-existent weight.
Two angels flank the head though show
no interest in a subterfuge.

This replica – a sturdy boy
who died too young too many years
ago – held a likeness lost for
his familiars till the fake corpse
got shipped beyond the grievers to
a future chipped and casual, eyed
by strangers sometimes in a place
admittedly he worshipped in
while he not here nor anywhere
is present somewhere we can't know
or guess at (with perhaps his dog).

Home in Hot Summer
for Lynn

Up from our deep back garden glancing to
a cloudless sky dark blue when June's warm there
a plane describes a straight white line whose long
trail melts along the same and silent time
then vanishes towards a south-west sun
across the sea.

        Above in shadow from
the house two spotted *skippers* whirl against
each other, split apart, return till one
alights on a flat leaf quite near me to
display its fans though shuts them so it seems
to disappear but flies away again
alone.

        One gull floats motionless from no –
where to another unseen area
quite swiftly while far higher swifts dart to
and fro then leave to find more emptiness
in somewhere else like him.

            There've been two months
now – simply passing by and flickering –
some butterflies seen suddenly here, there,
in foliage who obviously don't wish
to hang around.
        They flit away too fast:
a paler yellow one than *brimstone*; one
all azure, tiny; one as reddish though
not jagged like a *comma*; and a fourth
with speckles of a different colour all
un-nameable for me but quite delightful.

Landscape Through Hail

for Lynn

Four minutes and the path was white while
fresh grass and the odd frail daffodil
hissing under hail guarded their green
and yellow. Tall slopes to either side
of this river-valley faded, veiled
by a chill descent continuous
in no wind. Far fleece of budded trees
gone subtly grey (a lighter grey than
the sky) like a photograph taken
elsewhere by some long dead relation
and lying forgotten in a clasped
leather album. Our boots crushing small
ice-pearls left prints hastily filled up
by the pelting fall. It would be hard
to track us, even prove we'd been here.
Nothing to conceal. Only to make
less definite. We formed a centre
moving through the same blurred constancy –
a scene by Hokusai with English
alders. All changed. Unreal. A cold
gauze curtain drawn across everywhere.
The frozen path veering from swirling
water – still black, absorbing the drop
of pellets as if they didn't count –
came to an end leaving uncertain
distance beyond the branches to blend
the hail reluctantly with farewell.

Leaves

in the Marianne North Gallery of Kew Gardens

i.m. Rory McEwen

Such delicacy such
precision
could only come
from love
botanically speaking

The flowers of course
rose
      tulip
           fritillary
apparently in three dimensions
petal behind petal
and also glowing
onions
      an artichoke
               red pepper caught and carved

    "True Facts From Nature"

But the leaves…
picked up wherever
studied for colour
ragged edges
wear (also tear)
catching dry light
you almost hear the rustle
as one gets blown along an ordinary road
and Rory pursued it
fixed it on vellum
and it proceeds to die

He gave pure transience
a lasting life
painstaking beauty
meticulous
but free as well with just
a touch of nonchalance

One stands in wonder
paying a debt
to art beyond art
a record of delight

Links from a Forgotten Chain

in pools where vapour-trails, rain-clouds,
blue vacancy stay relatively still
branches and hovering kestrels ape
more accurately what's been walked beneath
but in reverse – high language may
conceal discrepancies when colours leave,
shapes alter, former echoes don't
even disturb the cobwebs – noon slicing
between two houses lets a beech
partially obscured glow like a copper
cloud which could never have drifted
that low this early now – most galaxies
speed outwards to create in time
the space they'll subsequently move through – vague
terrain it's nowhere and belongs
to no-one always – yaffle-tap on trunk
quick, hollow, so familiar
although the wood's no longer there – the calm
lake of chromatic gracefulness
both after and before the whirl and flaunt -
valse too hectic to be danced to
save elf feet over a clovered floor – black
helicopters clattering as
they cross long ago lands of faërie
longed for, sometimes believed in, known
to be there not here never to be there –
Debussy's church-bells filtering through
the foliage – the sound of moonlight on
quays, rivers, eastern temples – white
hail heavy on unseen gardens – you will
find in an upper room beneath
the bed a sack of spurious gold – a kiss

as firework – sunlight on late moss –
refracted light, the bright fritillary
decays to dust, illusion gone –
a distant conflict bombshells lost among
the hiss of reeds – a phantom crow
floating above translucent lupins (it's
a photograph the shaman took
why not believe it?) – these are only facts
and facts aren't poetry unless

Marooned

Shipping one oar you let the small craft scrape
a rock some fifty inches high, no more
than sixty-seven feet in length, dark grey
and jagged-edged. The early evening sky
spread as a metalled ceiling, low, no lamp,
no rafters, pallid khaki, stretching to
infinity. No whys for dreams once they
go claustrophobic, half-surreal or not,
twisting their futures from the unforeseen.
You said to so I left the boat to crouch
on that harsh tiny island. Had I stood
I would have hit my head. You pulled away.
Twilight was blurring what had hitherto
been liquid distance disconcertingly.
The circle of horizons glowed as though
in mutiny. There was no sign of land.
On all fours, both palms bleeding now, I watched
the way you rowed and tried to see if you
were sad or smiling while I heard the sound
of oars grow fainter. Then you merged to dusk.
The air held still, filling with nothing save
the lapping of salt water on bare rock.

Non-Communication

The Tempter came by night so silently
I hadn't noticed its approach but then
immortals in whichever guise will tend
to stroll through space and time leaving no sound
behind no tell-tale footprint (hoofprint?) trace
of some missed presence and it brought me you
fake insubstantial so alluring three
dimensions once again though underneath
a golden sky instead of ceiling oh
only a dream-bewilderment well that's
its job deception making me incur
more chillingly the arid fact you're not
now hitherside the grave I wept of course
mourning such memories that avenue
of cedars stumbled up simply because
you'd touched my spread hand on that sofa's back
perhaps in anxious readiness who knows
a spark of intimacy flaring to
ignite what stayed unlabelled up till then
but not to get translated into word
or glance from either as we left that room
with blurred hope not quite certain where to go
and yet some subtle lodestone drew us through
the darkness to your eighteenth-century flat
where we would reinterpret all we'd thought
we were before and realise at last
you'd handle me the way I'd handle you
and then years later when we hadn't met
for far too long you feared by telephone
your niece would find *post mortem tuam* not
then even close at hand for heaven's sake

a letter I'd composed in florid terms
to capture details lost along the way
once passionate reality had shrunk
to what the eye recalled the skin retained
and casual helpers of the riven word
lurking somewhere behind your brow and mine
might muddle up their archives and omit
the crucial textures hallowed at the time

"J'écris pour ceux qui ont compris"

Not true as such. The pen instructs
its owner who gets led down lanes
I never knew existed or
imagined once. There was a dream.
People I recognized went by,
ignored me with a passing smile,
the ghosts of days grown mouldy in
that echoing room. It emptied as
I strolled around bewildered most
unhappy past tall windows, found
an open one from which a flight
of narrow steps insisted I
climbed down to a dark alley where
I waited wondering whether to
go this or that way, were they more
than mist-draped somewheres lost in time,
blurred destinations not to be
relied on so I stood alone,
longed to go back, desired to wake
up, stayed and sometimes am still there.

Paul Nash

                    If you stare hard
that cloud could be a flint
too weighty to pass through
any jagged valley
so why should these tree-trunks
pock-marked like megaliths
surprise you? Sunk for some
millennia, even
a forest has turned to
stone in Arizona
littering the sand slopes
with shards of bark.
                    Try these
then: pyramids in lieu
of breakers, green harbour
introducing trawlers
to a hotel foyer,
leaves hefty as rotting
fungi , locomotive
making an unscheduled
halt in a suburban
fireplace somewhere, one blank
wall mimicking a cliff
and vice versa.
                    Or
equinoxes equipped
with blurred suns, blue poplar,
that mirrored eagle with
his back to us, phases
of coast and planets, downs
crowned with beeches bleeding

into each other like
brown sponges shouldering
the moon away.
                    Along
adjacent clumps of mist
and distant cumulus
brought near, these landscapes lie
for dreams to form. Sunflowers
big as mill-stones hurtle
via soft gold and off-
pink to twist the seasons
one by one to something
never seen.

Pine Fog

for Lynn

no shadows here as you and I drift by
these glistening trunks no faun to glimpse as high
as sight goes even though a jay's just shrieked
from one invisible red branch no sound
at all while fallen needles muffle what
we tread on passing deathpale mushrooms so
cannot become penumbra now walk as
two phantoms of our former selves keep on
moving in mist outside the wood we're in
where distance slopes quite gently on one side
down greenery to reach a curtain moist
and grey which isn't there will also slide
away as we approach from mist when on
the further other side a similar
obtrusive non-existent really wall
won't do more than confuse our bearings for
a while each way letting us look back at
a forest leaving us with neither north
nor west for certain no sun overhead
no wind to shift a fog for an hour or so

Possibilities

It takes a batch of no time to reach no-
where. Those designs wished on us by the Fates
can manufacture cubes of fog to go
around the skull as if one meditates

alone to no avail. That seems unfair
and our fault always. Can mere vanity
help us don Donatello's David's care-
less smile and poise pretending modesty

when large grey birds disturb a twilight laid
for us to brood in walking, fall perhaps
in garden-ponds unfilled by lilies, drown

just for a moment? Dreamers would have stayed
beneath such shallow water till the laps
they made it flutter with have settled down.

Presence of Animals

To-day in daylight at eleven-five
a.m. we saw a thin fox run across
the road ahead but buildings, spread for miles
each way in all directions, leave no space
for fields or woods or burrows dug nearby.
What was he dashing to or from? We know
about our urban foxes lurking in
thick flowerbeds in some city gardens or
who lope through night from square to pavement, make
weird noises for the sleepless ones to smile
and wonder, sometimes peer from windows as
a darkened reynard slips past with no fear.

We even hope he'll stay now carefully since
some cruel and thoughtless layabouts begin
now it's October to make dogs (not "hounds"
they're dogs, just dogs) slay fleeing foxes, deer
and otters while the other vicious twerps
get slaves to force young pheasants closer to
their guns and build a smelly pile of dead
and wounded birds they actually regard
as clever. Loathsome lot. Just like the rich
repellent halfwits go to Africa
and pompously stand somewhere safe so they
can shoot another lion then smirking stand
on its warm carcase for a photograph.

In Search of Lost Time

A girl I fancied in the fifties
(not a Gilberte nor an Albertine
and they were transposed boys anyway)
pronounced his name to rhyme with Faust. She
also rode a motor-bike.
            A friend's
beautiful mother wanted to go
to Glyndebourne but her first syllable
chimed with sinned not mind. Never mind. No
sin involved. I referred to a bird
in someone's cage as budge-ERRI-gar
and called the handsome Greek ADD-on-iss
more than once. A talk on Hugo I
gave at Reading included my dire
use of PROSE-oddie for prosody
corrected quietly while my ears blushed
a fetching scarlet.
            How to capture
Marcel's prose (without the "oddie")? So
complex, rich, contorted with his aim
of snaring the truth of love in most
exquisite elaboration. In
one New Year, alone at Cambridge, I
read all *A la recherche* in the old
nrf edition in sixteen
tomes (castigated by Beckett as
"abominable" in that long essay
where he sought to catalogue times when
"the boredom of living is replaced
by the suffering of being" – what
a cheery adage to be going

on with) but at the moment I am
re-reading the Pléïade edition
in only three leather-bound volumes
and, yes, Cocteau and Gide were correct
charging Proust with cowardice – all those
dishy but improbable female-
butchers and bearers of telegrams
were a dishonest disavowal
of his desires. *Sodome et Gomorrhe*
is sordid more than joyous (unlike
Un Ami dort or *L'Immoraliste*)
though reading between the lines you learn
that Saint-Loup forms the author's ideal
male.
        Still. It's unfair to cast a stone.
Society would turn against him
and society was what he'd set
out to dissect. So wittily too.
Those crisp dialogues brilliantly
let the speakers give themselves away
with lust, snobbery or prejudice.
There are longueurs but as with Wagner
you need them as slow preparation
for each dramatic launching into
that many-coloured empyrean
where fire makes Elstir's sunsets, rivers
reproducing clouds cut châteaux off
from longing and a breeze can carry
scents from hawthorn to identify
remembrance like a loose flagstone or
the taste of a madeleine in tea.

Too arcane? Too lengthy? Too abstruse?
Well, rewarding too, like some others:
Finnegans Wake? (*A way a lone a*

last a loved a long the back to where
we came in which proved *the most leavely
of leaftimes*). Or *La Vie mode d'emploi*?
(Molinet painted *avec brio*
portraits both of Elstir and Bergotte).
Erlöschung? (Eight hundred pages in
two paragraphs. Outstripping Faulkner,
Broch and Pinget!)
                            The joy of reading
might be menaced now in many ways
but Proust has bolted Time to Chance so
firmly we must concur the only
real paradises are the ones we've
lost and all discoveries now become
"*fugitives, hélas! comme les années*".

Revelation

The bare cathedral stripped of pews
a columned barn with strips of sunlight

walking where people sat

space

side-chapels emptied too
bare floor
no altar rail no brocaded hassocks
stone bench against the wall
my spine not touching red flowers
painted there five hundred years ago

gazing at emptiness through emptiness
an emptiness full of something more than air
than light
than scent of lilies
than memories hovering above each tomb
than shadows when jackdaws pass the window

a voice unspoken
to clarify the inexplicable

                    "nothing but God"

St. Gabriel's Chapel, Exeter Cathedral, July 8th 2012

Since

The sun broke through in time to grieve
or make the sacred larches flame
not burn since false assessments leave
a landscape never quite the same
since subtle brush-strokes let the lane
look tarnished and some cornfields ripe
since yesterday seem green again
but won't affect the words which wipe
damp tears from mourners' cheeks each time
the churchyard's left in shadow since
a weight once propped against the heart
means sympathisers think in hints
chilled and unwelcome from the start
as any poisoned nursery-rhyme

Farewells to those who've passed at last
to the unknown forever brought
black lightning from a sky these there
had quite forgotten since they'd thought
they walked undangered from the past
since witnesses weren't anywhere
though some among them clung to fact
and probed beneath each repartee
revealing with unwonted tact
a vultured curiosity
since after all the dead have gone
and took their secrets with them missed
of course but silent counting on
suns always curtained by grey mist

Romantic

At home nowhere but happy here
or there when things look settled
for a while – only a while
since otherwhere is always beckoning,
the grass more emerald, windows
far brighter, stars relied on.

To-morrows come though not in vain.
Rain only falls between the stroke of mid-
night and pre-daybreak. When you've been too
long somewhere restlessness sets in and you're
away again and no-one can
identify the destination, that's the key.

Sunlit Wandering
Wednesday in Holy Week 2014

To find the solitude – a field
perhaps with one oak (gnarled of course)
guarding a tangled shadow, round now, which
gets stretched from noon on till there's one long streak
of thin grey over evening grass
while foliage on the south-west side
catches the dying gold.
          Beyond
a gate the unused quarry-floor's
sparse with Chaucerian daisies. On
the rough-hewn cliff – brown, glossy black
in parts – a birch points up the rock-
face like a mast in triumph. To
walk on, glimpse hills in distance draped
harsh yellow. Now volcanoes *did*
form hereabouts æons ago
but that's not sulphur cooling, just
rapeseed. Crossing a crater once
in north-east Iceland where the ground
feels paper-thin (and warm) I saw
such colour, evil, steaming.
          Here
in Devon under April you
can suffer premonition of your death,
a slip from what's familiar to a blank
unknown. No irises, no books,
no wine, no amber ear-rings chosen for
my daughter's birthday. Exile to the dark
before what happens next or how –
a period in the void to reach
the right to Paradise? Forget

so much to gain much more. Lost in
the Arctic maybe where the sun
(when visible) stirs hardly to
and fro. No east no west. Curved space
and ice. So if a pole stood there
its drawn-out shadow wouldn't shrink
from dawn to midday like the one
this poplar casts.
                        To-day's the eve
of Passover when prophecies
get ratified, some prayers are said
through salt and blood, friends fail to stay awake,
a traitor plants his kiss. To-day
the planet holds its breath, seems to
be scattering hope and sunlight – air
a sacred blue – that sloping wood
mimicking sky with bellflowers – all
trees hung with birdsong – overhead
larks rivalling each other.
                        Down
on angled meadows wary calves
try out their hoofsteps. Startled lambs
veer capering. The sun-filled scene
must darken for them too, ourselves
as well eventually though not
all being well as imminent
as Friday's blackened afternoon
just two days on.
                        To skirt the shade
beneath unswaying branches, tread
lit grass attempting to avoid
the lady-smocks and celandines,
ignore the watch-face on the wrist,
step outside time, rely on all

that's plucked from times of wandering
to hoard for lifetime still unsolved.

These are some ways of looking at
a shredded future in uncertain spring
with a light breeze and surer memories
of what seemed worth it in the past
and may have been at that. Who knows?

Sunset

they know it's going down they know
dark will soon stay until what's bright
comes back that way
                              there
                                        some now fly
around in flocks uncertain where
to choose a branch though others dart
more carelessly
                         turn quick as all
moves towards silence from those scraps
of warning
                    meaningless
                                   self praise
as colour alters
                       blurs shine
                                      needs
to brush away the easier path
of day
          red doesn't stay too long
blurs also
                slightly vanishes
its silence spreads more eerily
to quench the property of light

The Approach of Future

A babe wakes as sunrise
illuminates the room –
death's a day nearer

The schoolgirl with satchel
waits for the eight-ten bus –
death's a day nearer

The student past midnight
has finished the essay –
death's a day nearer

The nurse comes with breakfast
along the sleepless ward –
death's a day nearer

The pilot lifts the plane
above grey morning clouds –
death's a day nearer

The farmer strolls across
his yard, opens the barn –
death's a day nearer

I'm shaving on Sunday
the service starts at eight –
death's a day nearer

Look back to the lost past.
Life came to some and us,
stays with a memory

We move from night to day
and back with some interests –
when's a tricky word

The Forest Path
Above the Teign in June 2014

Leaving the swift river far below
dims its turmoil against the rocks

Between the trees up here lies silence
a silence undisturbed
by sweeter other sounds from countless birds
unseen
warning or rejoicing who can tell

A ring of red on one trunk
(a "fell pine" like one in some German tale
harbouring of course a dragon
never glimpsed in the shadows)
to be felled by a sawyer before
it fell of its own accord

This path a gentle steepness
leads to a jutting hillfort
not especially of interest just
a round of dip and wall
the centre drowned in bracken
so good to walk to
passing views cut in the forest
to display on the river's other bank higher
than where you're standing
a clump of firs on the long summit
sheer sheet of green dropping to the river
outcrops of granite
four deer one white unworried by the slope

Hard to explain the pleasure
after all
a moving landscape
sky with slow clouds
two drifting buzzards
foxgloves small mushrooms speedwells
teasing vistas
        that
is all it is

The Last Intruder

My name? I have a crowd of names but feel
I'm known by what I do not who I am.
I took the lovely princeling in his prime
and ripped the blossom from that apple-tree.
I work with harm and metal, frost and blood,
despair, starvation, acid and disease.
I filch their hope from captives, draw dry clouds
across the sky of charity and send
some voyages on a fatal course. I braid
the hangman's cord for him, stack faggots for
the pyre and hone the axe-blade for a man
whose black mask covers half his face.
                                    I can
be utterly relied on, take no bribes,
am never late. Sometimes I've come too soon
causing a dark surprise but that was not
through eagerness. I work unhurriedly,
impartially, content when what's decreed
gets carried forward without bungling, fuss,
distraction or complaint.
                          No sympathy –
that's vital – I can't act against myself
while aiming viciousness at life or growth
with sudden violence or slow decay.

I'm deaf to pleas, excuses, alibis
and mercy is a vacant word for me.
My rôle's to deal out destinies – red knaves
or aces on the green baize table – though
without the benefit of chance because
the losing card you pick was always yours.

The Long Castle

for Lee, fellow-mountaineer and -maker of dreams

You and I planned to go the whole way.
Friends showed photos of parts in ruins,
warned us stretches of the wall weren't there
any more. This did not dissuade us.
No poet's scared to walk along long-
distance truth – or paved myths come to that.
Its length is anyway a matter
for dispute. We didn't mind straying
sometimes into Han from Ch'in, checking
northern cypresses against red cliffs
at evening. Remember when we met
the ghost of General Ch'i Chikuang
at the Flowery Tower? He said once we'd
clambered up the Heavenly Ladder –
more hazardous than Crib Goch because
man-made – we'd see the palace lanterns
glimmering across forty miles. There,
the sages stroked their white beards, sipped cups
of pale wine and watched the moon before
inking a brush to set a poem
down

> *high on the battlements*
> *waiting until snowfall*
> *memories of the peach-tree*
> *and grey geese on the pond*

(Pastiche of course, dear friend. Look. No hands.)
There's a pool there, too, fed by two springs,
one steaming, one icy, Mongolia
to our right across rougher terrain.
The General assured us horses

could walk five abreast further on. Here
the wall's too narrow, set with staggered
apertures for warriors to lie
or kneel or stand to shoot attackers.
He pointed out the Beacon. "One wisp
of smoke, one gunshot means a hundred
men on their way." Strange arithmetic,
we thought, but there were fine bas-reliefs
of lotus-blossom carved not far from
the Terrace for Mustering Officers.

You know none of this ever took place.
I'd found again the lovely guide-book
my sister gave us after "doing"
the Great Wall and the terracotta
army. She got back to Beijing when
that student was defying the tanks.
The hotel staff piled into her room
to watch the protest on CNN.
The authorities weren't letting it
appear on party-controlled TV.

Confecting dreams requires a certain
blend of bland reportage and shameless
fantasy – cold eye and flaming pen.

Before the maple-trees in the curved
stone valley turn crimson we must climb
that flight of steps on hands and knees, pause
out of breath and, looking at those towers
studding distance to infinity,
think of all those dead philosophers
who fell asleep long before the moon
had slipped beyond a dark horizon.

The Visitor

Those shapely limbs and torso tanned
from one long Grecian summer gave
the game away – he must have sun-
bathed naked, loins a purer gold
from crotch to navel proving where
white trunks had rarely been.
                                     He strolled
around the house that wasn't his
with nothing on, then twenty seemed
much younger, tricky to assess,
may well at times have been asked to
pose as a junior god not done
in marble, mortal, mobile, more
like an ephebe dried by a wind
off The Aegean, standing there
his veins tinged with some Bacchic blood
lending that hint of danger – poised
and fleet – no wings to either heel.

To be preciser could appear
too near the knuckle and that's not
the part of the anatomy
the other, older, banked on when
he saw him on the threshold clothed
and smiling while the early leaves
of autumn fluttered round.
                                    He said
he'd stay a day, no more, went north,
swore that he'd send his new address
and never did.

There's just the taste
imagined of retsina in
his kiss and tiny olive-groves
along the distance of his smile.

Three People Then Four

Invited to the Embassy of France
in Tôkyô two friends, a journalist
who writes such lovely poetry and a man
of many possibilities sat down
with me and three filled glasses to drag back
the world to rights round one small table in
a spacious room with elements which hold
nostalgic hints of Paris and the Loire.

We chatted, drank and in those far-off days
smoked *High Right* (then we three were in Japan)
called cigarettes and, puffing, spoke not to
argue for fun, just questioned quietly with
lips pursed or lifted brow but always showed
true understanding from the pleasant past,
relieved to be together once again
in such a place
                    when someone passing stopped,
looked at us, laughed in a keen interest
not snobbishly but with a sense of warmth.
The journalist asked where's the joke and smiled.
The laugher stopped, apologised then said
"You're all good linguists but it's rather odd
to hear a Frenchman talking English while
an Englishman is speaking Japanese
and one born here chats fluently in French."

Our jaws dropped, we gazed up at him, looked round
each other and burst out in helpless mirth.
"Sit down" I said and rose. "What language now
would you prefer while I'm away to fetch

what you might want to drink? Wine? Beer? Champagne?"
He gestured to a distant table. "No.
"No, no. Most kind. I'm over there with them."
I dared to say "I'm Welsh, born in Penarth"
and coughed, then switched: *"ima watakushi wa*
Yokohama kokuritsu daigaku
no kôshi desu."
"I realised" he said
and laughed once more. Joyly we three joined in.

(P.S. Translation: "I'm now a lecturer at Yokohama National University"
(there are others there).

Week Weak or Not

According to the watch my kind wife gave
me (we once tried a shop in London where
an armed thug watched a nicer man display
a rather ugly wristwatch which would cost
seventeen thousand quid we said "Well, well"
and went to try elsewhere) to-day is called
Mon One on the watchface which sounds just like
Chinese for something but could mean gold coins
win over any prudent thought.
                              Wed Three
hints counting and adultery, tut, tut,
my parents wouldn't smile at that but then
divorces in those days were few and far
between not so this century.
                              Fri Five's
the sort of beastliness jihadists (what
a name) get up to frequently and they'll
hurl males who love males (and why shouldn't they)
down from high roofs or is it rooves. All those
who breed such works of horror have no right
to be dubbed human beings.
                              Sat Six shows
meek pride for a long sofa in a room
too big for us to house.
                              Sun Seven may
welcome an unsuspected lad to join
the other six (and are there daughters?)
                              May
lifts this spring month to summer so why have
Tue Two (true too?) and *Thu Four* (therefore?) been
left out? That thatchered mimic May may rue

"therefore" and *"to"* for all her to-ing plus
her brex-ing round the continent we're told
to break from.

          Wait till Junes bring one or two
ripe answers whether each new week seems weak,
days daze and years may bring us tears to stay.

Like Autumn

At 59 I gave up teaching French
and German, later Japanese as well.
Retirement! Chance to find more novelties?
Not true. There's somehow never time to do
what's better than the chosen chore. We have
gone off to places we'd not yet explored –
Honduras, Egypt, Crete, Tunisia,
Morocco, Portugal, Bolivia,
Guatemala, Jordan, Costa Rica,
Peru and Mexico. (I went alone
to Iceland twice to look in awe at those
high waterfalls, stand on the glacier
under Eyjafjallajökull, walk across
bare stretches of volcanic rock still warm
to timid feet.) We didn't have the gift
of gab to anyone or where, got round
with pigeon-Spanish, learned a twisted O
is 5 in Arabic and searched the Greek
for loo.
         Five days a week I wrote on black-
boards, spoke and read three alien tongues (English
as well) for decades. After taking off
the gown and cap I never wore I kept
on savouring Proust, Kafka and Ryôta
but rarely *talked* or *scrawled* in lingoes I'd
so long so much enjoyed. Old age crept in
almost unnoticed and one day I gazed
stunned at *chardons* in one of Balzac's books.
I had to look it up. "Thistles". I winced.
Never before had his *Illusions*
been so *perdues*.

In recent years I've lost
words Rilke used and can't remember – let
alone write stroke by stroke – the ideographs
that clarified the next town on the train
to Yokohama University
four times a week.
             Depression came because
I'd loved to curl my English thoughts into
the languages I'd learned so made my way
again through lists and conjugations, tried
quite hard to memorise them all and (when
alone) recite a sonnet by Ronsard,
a speech from Grillparzer's *Weh dem, der lügt!*
and haiku by Bashô and Shiki. These
have worked and stayed but gaps that crouch in all
four sentences grow vaster week by week.
In chats with people I can't suddenly
bring words to mind, names, what has been in fact
just mentioned – *clover, Heimat, voluntary,*
aubaine, deter, Gotanda, reprimand,
Brecht, mulberry, kabuki, camouflage,
appendix, perpendicular.
                    I watch
their faces waiting frozen while I try
to ransack what's been left in cubbyholes
along the brain, often to no avail.
They look so patient, condescending, think
"*oh, poor old boy*".
                As things get worse, as there's
more gloom, as I perceive all losses will
be there to stay and multiply, there's been
a sort of giving-in, a cowardice,
a feeble grip on logic and I see
each little phrase, each once-loved memory
detach itself like autumn leaf from branch

and flutter down the wind or sunlight with
a certain sadness since December will
decide the closure and now all around
in space and night and time there stays a sense
of resignation meaning no return.

Argument

All poetry's just fiction.
Balls!

Those too
(two) do display their half-existence when
joy's not required. Some poets speak of death
as though they'd been there, wandered round, seen grey
unruined castles looking better than
they're now, chatted with ghostly heroes who
stand by each black not flowing river, saw
such wonders all may see on fatal days.
Some others have preferred to waste a page
inventing human futures on a moon
that spins round Jupiter. Such gibberish.
All wishful dreaming, no reality,
false maps which fail to show you where you are
or where you want to go to, promises
left unfulfilled.

But think. The penmanship.
Those gifts of newness. Words in black on white
stay put and can't be queried. Keats gives us
(please note I use the present tense) a star
so steadfast; De la Mare says look on all
things lovely every hour; Lee Harwood proves
no adjectives can match those colours on
the ocean; Frost stood still and stopped the sound
of feet while Browning lets del Sarto tell
us how a man's reach should exceed his grasp
or what's a Heaven for? Anne Stevenson
perceives a cloud which Constable'd not seen
and quotes Old Ez. No poet can walk, think
and write at the same magic time. They have

to ponder, keep the glow safe and spend months
sometimes attacking lexicons to lift
those certain moments from the past.
                                        Untrue.
That star's not there at noon. The stroller moves
away. The sea's obliterated by
a sudden fog. One rose lets petals loose,
scent's lost in winter. Skies on canvas hang
opaque. Frustration can't be comic.
                                        Yes
it can. Attempts to catch the swaying of
a poplar make a poet smile as he
recalls some palm-trees in a hurricane
and Flaubert's *mot juste* after weeks of trial
finds sober writers capering in a graveyard.

No Books No Writers No Future

The past keeps dwindling since some sadly un-
dereducated teachers teaching now
too many lazy adolescents
                    (who
can't read or won't because they haven't been
encouraged even forced to learn by heart
what seems at first quite difficult but does
with fascinating study twist to bliss –
expansion – newness – till the active world
of education proves to be a path
of light leading to other stranger ways
of confidence and tolerance also)
                    send
away from schools a flock of ignorant
and vapid human hardly beings who
should they choose teaching as a job would breed
a less informed, dull generation who'll
create one even sloppier and so
on.
        Hence a glance at lakeside sadness for:

There was a time when Chaucer, Marlow, Keats,
    Ronsard and each word Kleist put down
            To us then meant
    A slant on what we thought we knew,
The rapture and the challenge of discern.
It isn't now the way things used to be
        Since everywhere you find
        Much worthless verse,
Such pointless paintwork, rubbish strewn around called "Art".
    New novels come and go

Though most are not worthwhile.
These actors on the stage
Or screens can't talk so you can't hear.
Wallace Stevens, Yves Bonnefoy,
Plus Derek Walcott gave
Like Klee, de Staël, Rothko all
The splendour of modernity
And luckily a few've survived to hold the sun.

Thanks to the readers of the thrilling past,
Thanks to its themes and sly discoveries,
To us the rustle of a former page
Lends untold pleasures streaked with happy tears.

A Quarter-Paradise?

The King had died. An unsplit country mourned
    a monarch who'd stayed put throughout
the war. Broadcasting House chose nothing but
    silence and solemn music. No
slick commentators, pointless interviews
    with egos who don't matter.
                                    Two
p.m.
        The nation held its breath for two
    whole minutes. There's a photo of
Trafalgar Square. Hundreds of subjects are
    all standing still, not glancing at
each other, some with heads bowed, others just
    remembering a man not born
to be a king. He'd reigned because it was
    his duty – nothing more than that –
and through a stammer won respect. Eighteen,
    at Cambridge, moved, I still wore like
my friends a mask of feigned indifference.
    All day long we rehearsed a play.

The Wales and England which I knew and loved
    have now dissolved beyond recall.
Real life then wasn't cynical or flip.
    Politeness mattered. People queued.
You didn't use foul language on the street
    or walk in public semi-nude
flaunting obscene tattoos or plonk your feet
    up in the bus. We had much more
in common like those Ealing comedies
    (and even Gainsborough Pictures). There

were witty *songs*, words you could understand
　　unamplified *and tuneful too* –
home-grown or from the U.S.A. The B
　　BC's three programmes (Home, Light, Third)
catered for all tastes. All one August I
　　worked on a market-garden. In
the tea-break we swapped jokes from *Goon Shows* or
　　Take It From Here. There yawned no gap
between the young and old created by
　　commercial plotting. Children weren't
brainwashed by vested interests and at school
　　(facing the blackboard sensibly)
learned facts from teachers who knew how to spell.
　　Footballers had a day-job not
some pricey mansion, didn't sport a shirt
　　plastered with some advertisement,
weren't bought and sold for sums no-one deserves
　　(not even bankers). Who is worth
a million pounds? Why is there never cash
　　enough for hospitals or schools
or libraries but plenty for a war?

　　And sportsmanship – the will to win
gracefully,　smiled acceptance of a wrong
　　against one, the ability
to lose without a snarl. To watch a match
　　with joy in skills one lacks, not vexed
or thrilled by the result, just pleased to see
　　the players do what's far beyond
one – like delight (with envy) as a Bach
　　fugue gets untangled with such ease
by someone mercifully not Glenn Gould.
　　One laughs with Stephen Potter from
the standpoint of the opposite although
　　with Lifemanship pomposity

becomes the victim with pretentiousness
and snobbery so one tends to join
the other side and cheer the culprit on.
    But then sports aren't important like
the arts – as long as honesty comes first:
    think of that vile female who on
the stands at Wimbledon shone in the eyes
    of X from a held mirror so
her favoured Y would win. You saw this caught
    on television. No-one seemed
to mind or even notice her foul act.
    No guard came up to challenge her,
drag her down all those steps and throw her on
    the street. Why not though?
                            Long before
the Age of Murdoch, Eden lied about
    the Suez crisis but, despite
attempts to muzzle them, broadcasts direct
    from Cairo told us how our 'planes
were dropping bombs. We heard behind the voice
    frequent explosions like the Blitz.

We didn't have those cardboard cut-outs dubbed
    "celebrities" back then. There were
the Dockers and their like to ridicule.
    True fame got earned by bravery,
fine craftsmanship, achievement, even charm
    evinced as inborn and sincere.
Actors enunciated – even knew
    what the words meant. On Oxford Street
a cinema showed foreign films. *Fin de*
    Partie was broadcast on the Third –
in French! It took more than an hour. I got
    roped in by Michael Bakewell to
interpret for Jean Martin (later doomed

to meet a sticky end inside
the Jackal's violent day) and Roger Blin
    as Hamm who'd dared to warn Orphée
one should not know how far to go too far.
    Though thrilled I heard no talk of art –
they merely dreamed of schemes to pay no tax.
    Father was an inspector for
the Inland Revenue (how he'd despise
    that coinage 'taxman'). I possessed
no cunning tips to help them dodge the law.

    For Higher Cert. (Mod. Lang.) you read
at least eight texts like *Egmont* or *Le Cid*.
    That dropped to four. Then none. How can
you write or speak a foreign language till
    you've understood what have been held
for centuries the best ways to arrange
    a well-thumbed treasury of words?

To-day those who can't draw or paint or carve
    are called by "critics" (and some bland
museum-runners) *artists* – and, what's more,
    are praised – and paid! – for unmade beds,
dunked sharks, incompetence. Some subtle crooks
    behind the scenes manipulate
the gullible and profit handsomely
    from their con-tricks. "Come here and see
the naked emperor, gawp at his clothes –
    then pay me for them." Ah, where are
equivalents of Hitchens, Hepworth, Nash,
    Nicholson, Sutherland or Moore?

Poems get published which aren't poetry –
    mere diary-jottings, ego-trips,
limp propaganda without skill. No craft.

No music. "Now I'll read what I
wrote on the bus this morning." What a treat.

Back sixty years almost an age
of silver (not of gold): no mobile phones
    to interrupt a funeral or
soliloquies from *Hamlet*. No obese
    girls flashing navels, cars that blare
non-music *thumping THUMPING* (non-stop too
    in shops and cafés – even pubs).
No supermarkets (driving off small stores
    and helpful garages) put there
by evil councils. On Cheam High Street then
    a dairy; Surrey Motors; Hicks
the butcher; barber; sweetshop (ah, bull's-eyes);
    clothes-shop; Hicks the greengrocer (no
relation) who all through the War had in
    his window hanging a big bunch
of wood bananas; chemist; bookshop; *Helps
    Electric.*
            Now roads, railway-lines,
brash towns of plastic ugliness encroach
    on farmland. And so on.
                        Be fair.
Time's come across with many reasons to
    rejoice. CDs give Chopin with
no scratching. Chaps who fall in love with chaps
    don't go to prison now and hip-
replacements let us hobblers stroll again.
    Amazing cameras (once you've learnt
to use them) take as many pictures as
    you like – a full moon trapped within
the window of a ruined castle or
    a still-life in mosaic (grapes
and tulips) in Tunisia on the wall

of a superb museum where
photography's allowed. Lord Chamberlains
    can't censor dramas (though there have
been times one's wished he'd snipped away at Bond
    and Brenton). We have food and drink
undreamed-of in the so-called good old days.

    Which makes for pleasing laziness,
a fresh mobility, maybe re-thoughts.
    Thank Heaven it's a royal land still –
FID. DEF. if not IND. IMP. The Commonwealth
    runs better than the Empire though
the latter did much good despite its blunders.
    I would not wish to die in a
republic. Give us coronations which
    require regalia to explain
why each anointed sovereign holds an orb
    (a gold world with a cross for our
protection) and a sceptre with a white
    enamelled dove as paraclete.

Then fifteen silver trumpets echo praise
    from stone floor to ribbed vault, make stained
glass windows quiver slightly in the waves
    of sound stressing the kingdom's luck
in living under continuity –
    safe-conduct handed on again
(but spare us please some so-called pop star who'll
    insult the Abbey with his whining).
It's not "My country right or wrong" nor what
    those crass reporters claim about
these isles: "*We're better, older, funnier.*"
    "*More modest, too*". "*The envy of
the world.*" Such drivel drops the poor U.K.
    to a banana kingdom, twists

what's true into a target for disdain.
    A patriotic streak must not
become confused with blinkered thinking or
    with xenophobia. It means
"I like it here." That's all. A pair of boots
    worn but still wearable.
                      End with
a bird's-eye view. A threnody for this
    embattled kingdom with its hills
soft under rain. Shores (sand or pebbled) blurred
    by sea-fret, oak-woods creaking in
November gales. A Saxon barn alone
    and greying in an empty field.
Two adolescent cygnets dipping beaks
    to their slim stream. A rutting stag
stalking in silhouette, high up a slope
    of trees losing their leaves, to pick
a likely doe.
              This quarter-paradise?
    Once-other Eden? Saved? Or lost?